TRULY HOME

TAYLOR THAO HO

T | H

TAYLOR THAO HO

TRULY HOME

IS WITHIN YOU

ABOUT THE AUTHOR

Taylor Thao Ho

is a 25-year-old Entrepreneur, Researcher and a Graduate Student. Her mission is to inspire everyone through her eliciting stories and innovative mindset to guide them in finding their place in this world. Taylor's work explores the theme of growth mindset, love, personal journey, and self-improvement.

As a Houston native and Longhorn alumni, Taylor truly feels at home when she is surrounded by comfort of others', relaxed ambience of a Spa lounge, and welcomed by a strong coffee aroma entering a bookstore. In all, this is Taylor Thao Ho first poetry book she wrote, designed and self-published.

Connect with Taylor Thao Ho on all Social Media – Linkedin, Instagram, and Facebook.

ACKNOWLEDGMENTS

Thank you to all those who have crossed my path in the past 25 years. You all have provided me with great encouragement, support, and shared of moments throughout my journey. Your impact has inspired me to write this book, Truly Home.

This book is truly dedicated to my readers and everyone I have formed meaningful connections with. I am eternally grateful for all the extraordinary experiences that have helped contribute into this masterpiece. Please note that the characters and events in this book are fictional, and any resemblance to actual persons or events is coincidental.

To my readers, I hope my poems are relatable to your journey and empowering to your soul. Thank you for sharing and supporting my work across the globe.

TABLE OF CONTENTS

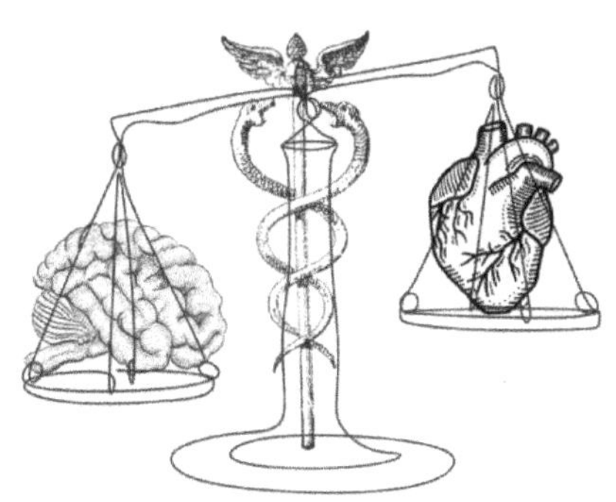

COMPASSION

T | H

COMPASSION

My heart is overflowin' with
genuine kindness
and compassion.

It's overflowin' with genuine
interest in others' lives,
heart-warmin' energy,
share of my wisdom and knowledge,
and impactin' others' lives.

COMPASSION

When you have healin' hands,
even the sickest person can get well.

Your healin' hands are
ready to give,
ready to cure,
and ready to heal.

The symptoms now come no more.

COMPASSION

Listen closely,
and hear through this.

Let me give you a hug,
allow you to freely express your feelings,
without criticism or judgements,
and give you a helpful point of view or two.

Just for you.

COMPASSION

Take time for more dialogue.

I know it might not come with ease when
sharin' your thoughts,
and feelin' vulnerable.

With time and communication,
will come with ease,
to getting' us through.

COMPASSION

Let me
spoil you,
bind you up,
care for you,
nurture you
when you're hurtin'.

Let me,
Show you the beauty in these spokes of life.

COMPASSION

To every cardiac arrest case,
I want to be a part of the rescue mission.

I desire to be...
The doctor that's there all day and night,
Fixin' and stitchin' the wounds away.

Let me be your healer,
a healer for all hearts and souls.

COMPASSION

When an organ works just like it should,
you can feel the rhythm.

Feelin' the rhythm
of your own heartbeats
and intuitions.

COMPASSION

In this world,
we're here to live out.

Live out our purpose,
fulfill our passion,
with all the endless love inside.

We might be different,
speak in different tongues,
and think with different nerves.

But in the end,
you're there for me,
and I'm here for you when you need me.

COMPASSION

Medicin' the body and heart,
it's the beginning of healin'.

Regardless,
where you go from here,
start today cause tomorrow can't wait.

Make your healin' mission crystal clear.

COMPASSION

In a storm of patients,
I will find my way through
the high and low waves,
the ones that are livin' in darkness,
bein' out of their minds and soul until 6 AM.

No matter what - make your battle mine to stand for.
Time will find a way,
for things that are meant to be conquered.

COMPASSION

We live in an empty world.
A world with superficial people
and materialistic things.

We don't know how to care,
or how to show compassion.

We lack empathy,
authenticity,
kindness,
compassion.

We are so empty,
livin' in an empty world.

COMPASSION

Tonight,
I'm cravin' for something sweet at home.
In the mood to make a batch of macadamia,
white chocolate cookies.

Love and compassion,
the secret ingredients to every luscious bite of my soft,
decadent,
curvy,
intensely, delicious cookies.

So buttery,
so creamy,
so warm.

So much love and compassion,
thoughts and creations in this batch of cookies.

COMPASSION

I love your compassion.
Meltin' all hearts like butter.

You're so much warmer
than anybody I know.

Warm and hard to resist,
like chocolate truffle.

COMPASSION

What truly make you
feel comfort at home?

Is it comfort from loved ones?
Or it the feelin' of belongingness?

COMPASSION

Our ink bleedin' dark and bold,
writin' our own stories
with the ink we once shared.

COMPASSION

Its your grits,
patience,
curiosity,
and compassion
ignitin' your passion.

COMPASSION

Your gifts and unique qualities
are admirable to those
you have crossed paths with.

Make your path part of a historical landmark.

COMPASSION

When you talk about your
fears and concerns,
it's always the truth.

Your truth,
love,
and compassion
that heals all wounds.

COMPASSION

Be patience with the journey you're meant to board on.

You're on the journey of self-exploration,
discoverin' self-compassion,
and reflectin' self-growth.

Your final travel destination is still unknown.
Keep explorin'.

COMPASSION

Only you can heal your broken heart.

Heal your deep wound,
heal your insecurities,
heal your self-doubts,
and heal your mindsets.

You are your own Cardiologist.

COMPASSION

Like the flowers in the garden,
it takes time to bloom one day at a time,

Untouched by any other growin' thing,
it takes supportive and compatible roots
to make a tree stand tall and deep,
enough sustain the wind.

Stay rooted in the storms and darkness.
Eventually,
you'll find your way bloomin' safely.

COMPASSION

Have you truly found
what you have been searchin' for?

You've been searchin' for the perfect home,
perfect man,
perfect career,
perfect friendship,
perfect car,
and perfect lifestyle.

But have you truly found
the perfectly imperfect you along the way?

P U M P I N' • B E A T S

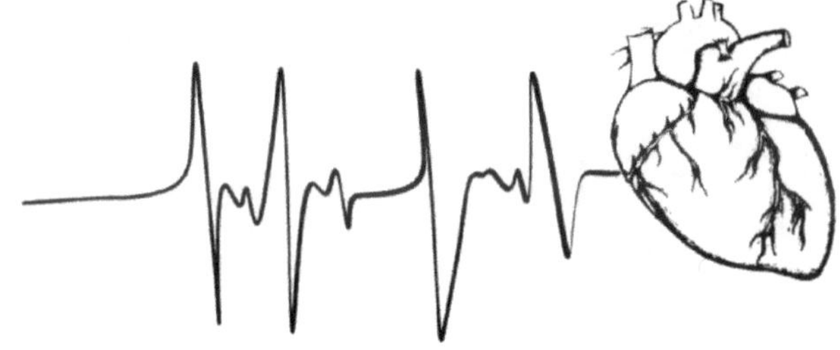

P U M P I N' • B E A T S

Better be cautious of what you say
to the lady in red.
The one in high heel shoes,
with luscious, cherry, red lips.

Ooh,
She's a dangerous,
beautiful lady.
A fallen angel she is.

Think you might break her heart?
She'll make you play with your own heart.

P U M P I N ' • B E A T S

I'm up against the world,
nothing is dimin' my pumpin' purpose
and no one ain't backin' down.

Oh,
you are so damn proud o' me.

P U M P I N' • B E A T S

Blood and passion,
Runnin' through my veins.

Feelin' so in control,
I have no fear of things that make out of control.

PUMPIN' • BEATS

The electrical impulse,
between you and me.

Our dreams and visions,
all over my mind,
triggerin' one heartbeat after another.

Feel the pulse beatin'?
Our futures are electrifyin'.

PUMPIN' • BEATS

Missin' home,
but I'm feelin' alright.

Bad days and good days,
where life just looks okay.
Strong days and weak days,
where it's just a fight of rhythms
and beats to stay alive.

Stayin' alive to do better the day before.

PUMPIN' • BEATS

Imagine your first heartbeat.

Young and hungry for life,
all you wanted was to be found.
Searchin' for your purpose and mission.
Half of it,
you have already found.
Other life,
still in search.

Learnin' to keep up the beat,
Loosenin' the vessel and let it flow.

PUMPIN' • BEATS

Heart valves openin' and closin'
connectin' with others' left and right,
all day and night.

Yet,
the blood in my heart's
still flowin' back to you.

PUMPIN' • BEATS

Life's been great.

I'm in it,
moment to moment.
I've seen the darkest of days,
and the lightest of lights.

Regardless if it's a battle or success,
the beats are still pumpin'.

P U M P I N' • B E A T S

Feel the electrifyin' moment tonight.

Let the signal travels down your His-Purkinje system,
and allow it to spread across your heart.

Feel the rhythms and beats of me,
tonight.

PUMPIN' • BEATS

Don't be a heart blocker.

You might affect the electrical impulses
travelin' through the heart,
affectin' you from lovin'
or acceptin' love from others.

So,
Don't be a heart blocker.

PUMPIN' • BEATS

There are stars in her eyes
makin' it harder to look at her.

Her energy is irresistible,
so magnetic,
glowin' from afar.

Her touch is icy yet full of warmth.
Her words flowin' smoothly,
makin' you addicted to her talk.
Pumpin' your beats,
after beats.

That's how dangerous she is to your heart.

PUMPIN' • BEATS

Goin' through the motion and flow,
Feelin' good is all that I want to feel.

I now have energy all through my veins,
I'm stronger than I ever been.

P U M P I N' • B E A T S

Love the taste of you in the mornin'.
Drippin' in cream,
so warm,
so silky.

Your smell,
a mixture of intoxicatin' bitter-sweet,
bloody vanilla,
and a sprinkle of seductive,
cinnamony spice.
So nuzzleable,
so delectably comforting,
fillin' up the excitement in the entire room.

Moisten my tongue with the creaminess,
boldness,
and sweetness of a Cappuccino as I sip.

This is all I need to pump and exhilarate my day.

PUMPIN' • BEATS

How thick are your artery walls?

Are your walls thick enough to withstand the pump?
The pumpin' of pressure,
The pumpin of rich-oxygenated blood
deliverin' to your cells.

Are your walls thick enough to secure all the promises?
Securin' the blood vessels,
Securin' our home through all blood storms.

How thick are your artery walls?

43

45

SECRET • VALVES

S E C R E T • V A L V E S

We have 4 valves.

The 4 valves of promise to the
Aortic,
Mitral,
Pulmonic,
and Tricuspid
in this lifetime.

Value your valves.

SECRET • VALVES

Hearin' melodies in my heart,
feelin' a bit unusual.

Emotions,
they're steamin' red hot like fever.
Leavin' the softest skin sweatin' to the bone.

It's a fever.
The mildest fever you've ever felt,
ignitin' the flame inside me,
for you to feel.

S E C R E T • V A L V E S

Move around with purpose,
and feel the fire,
in your souls.

Fuel your passion,
purpose,
compassion,
and secrets.

Have your future ready to rise
above the sparks and flames.

SECRET • VALVES

If I tell you all my secrets,
Will you hold me tight?

Promisin' to heal all those deep hidden scars?
Allowin' me to be who I always admired to be?

SECRET • VALVES

Fell in love idolizin' you,
from the screen afar.

Scrollin' through your profile,
hopin' you'll be mine.

SECRET • VALVES

There's a secret in the nighttime,
I can feel it.
Somewhere waitin' for me,
I know it.

Loneliness is only startin' to get to me,
The darkness has taken control.

SECRET • VALVES

I'm not just another person.
Not just another young, beautiful lady
you meet.

I'm rare.
So rare that you might try to find me,
in another person.

I expressed a plethora of emotions,
Felt a thousand times of love, loss, failures,
Been through days and nights.

There's no other way that built me,
for me.

S E C R E T • V A L V E S

Hold on a piece of my story,
Hold your thoughts of me close,
Hold on to what feels real.

Keep me safe and secure.

In hope,
we might meet again soon or
another lifetime.

For now,
keep searchin' for my light to guide you
out of the darkness.

S E C R E T • V A L V E S

Secrets,
They tell me your emotions.
I see them piercin' in your eyes,
all you want me not to see.

What are the secrets you're hidin'
Lies,
and disillusions
are crawlin' like a vine.

Hold yourself together,
with what's left of your pride.
Don't let them find out who you are
or you're about to lose it all.

S E C R E T • V A L V E S

It seems like everything I touch,
it heals all kind of wound.

Wounds that are always open and bleedin'
until I touch.

I heal and feel,
it all.

S E C R E T • V A L V E S

I feel like a stranger in my new home city.
Lonely,
Sad,
and full of uncertainties.

Take me back home.
To the place where I was born and raised.
To the place where I feel
Loved,
Supported,
And energized.

S E C R E T • V A L V E S

At night,
I wonder when this darkness will start fadin'.
Wonder when the city lights will guidin' the way for me.
I feel like a stranger in this city of mine.

Feelin' like I've wasted my time in this unknown,
and my mind still on you.
I feel like a stranger in this city of mine.

I need to stop feelin' like this.
It's time to make this new city
my home.

SECRET • VALVES

Different days,
Same valves,
flowin' the same blood.

SECRET • VALVES

Sorry if I'm slowin' down the flow.

I'm too busy flowin' in one direction,
too busy pumpin' beats,
too busy for time wasters,
too busy growin' my mindset,
too busy buildin' my empire,
and I'm too busy workin' on my body.

SECRET•VALVES

Perhaps,
our paths were meant to cross.

But not to continue developin' the highway.

SECRET • VALVES

You and I have secrets in common.

Shh,
Don't try to understand it.
It's a secret.

Secrets between us,
we're takin' it to heaven.

S E C R E T • V A L V E S

I only flow forward in life.

Flowin' from the body to the superior vena cava,
right atrium to the tricuspid valve,
right ventricle to the pulmonary arteries,
lungs to the pulmonary veins,
left atrium to the mitral valve,
left ventricle to the aortic valve,
aorta to the body.

I don't do backflow.

SECRET • VALVES

You carry the power of love.
The power of love is
inside your heart chambers.

SECRET • VALVES

24/7
Pumpin' and flowin'
Asleep or awake,
Your heart's faithfully loyal to you.

Keepin' you alive
another day and night.

SECRET • VALVES

She wears her confidence the same way
she puts on her red lipstick.
Bold,
allurin',
and seductive.

She accessorizes herself in diamonds
without lookin' at the price tag.
The same way she knows her worth.
Priceless,
valuable,
and rare.

Either you're compatible for her or
she won't make space for you.
Say you're leavin'?
Oh, she won't shed a tear.

Her heart truly knows
what it truly wants.

S E C R E T • V A L V E S

Never imagined flowin' smoothly across the vessels
and recreatin' another path.

Pursuin' hobbies and passions
I'd never dare.

Meetin' other cells from all walks of life,
and encounterin' beautiful valves along the way.

S E C R E T • V A L V E S

You'll flow forward in the direction of your connections.

Continue pumpin' the flow
to the valves,
and send electrical impulses throughout your heart.

69

ELECTRIFYING DISCOVERY

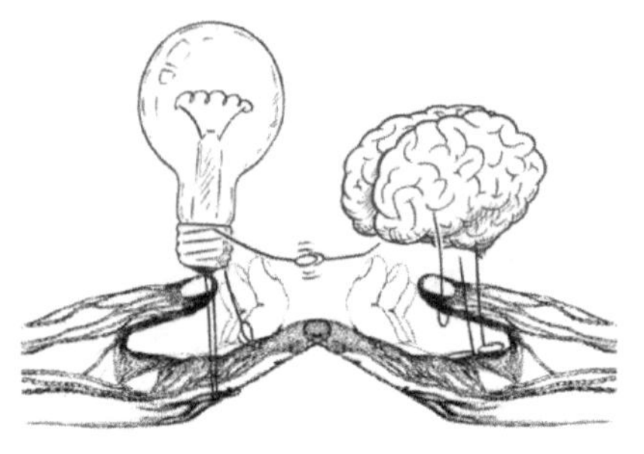

T | H

E L E C T R I F Y I N G • D I S C O V E R Y

The Universe's neuron
seems to be triggerin' with excitement,
tonight.

Sendin' me electrifying messages,
signals,
and all kind of signs.

ELECTRIFYING • DISCOVERY

Look up at the sky,
the journey is now chasin' me.

I'm the brightest star.
Glowin' my own way,
Catchin' my own stride,
And not dimin' down.

Discoveries are unravelin'
when it's me and only me by my side
if you're not the one meant for me.

ELECTRIFYING • DISCOVERY

I've always been discovered.

Ever since childhood,
discoverin' myself,
discoverin' my own mindset,
discoverin' my own passion,
and discoverin' my own growth.

ELECTRIFYING • DISCOVERY

It's amazin' how one moment
can capture all my attention.

I feel like it takes me to the next level,
so incredible,
so grateful
for all the moments.

If it weren't for amazin' experience,
I couldn't live a life worth livin'.

ELECTRIFYING • DISCOVERY

I don't need to find you,
I found myself in me.

Found myself in a thunderin' whirlpool
of intense passionate energy.
Where the surgical lights,
lightin' my soul's purpose.

I found me,
and I've never been more alive.

ELECTRIFYING • DISCOVERY

Night after night,
Coffee and sleepless nights.

Reinventin' myself as I'm
Dancin' in the moonlight
To keep my beautiful,
wild,
dreams
ignite and electrified.

ELECTRIFYING • DISCOVERY

Freedom of the mind is found in
Truth,
Integrity,
Ethics,
Passion,
And love.

Put yourself forward and upward,
To find your way.

Find your freedom.

ELECTRIFYING • DISCOVERY

Be confident in your own blood and bones.

Go,
wherever you go.

Be fine on your own,
always on your own.

Until the day you find me,
Keep walking one hundred thousand miles.

ELECTRIFYING • DISCOVERY

Find the strength
to be your soulmate.

Find the strength
that's never endin'

Find the soulmate in you.

ELECTRIFYING • DISCOVERY

A mind like a Ruby,
A heart like a Diamond,
A body like an Emerald.

Rare and valuable,
cannot be broken.

Now you know the worth
I'm worth.

I am a gem.

ELECTRIFYING • DISCOVERY

There's a new path created for me,
that I've just discovered.

I'm gettin' up.
Up,
and up.

Now as I'm standin' confidently,
No more self-doubts,
No more what-ifs,
No more waitin',
No longer the victim.

Unafraid,
I will rise and glow like a blazin' fire,
Growin' to be undefeated.

ELECTRIFYING • DISCOVERY

This discovery means so much,
so never try to take it for granted.

Don't walk away
when the fight of discoverin' yourself
is worth it.

Try and understand,
that you have all the confidence
in you.

ELECTRIFYING • DISCOVERY

I found something I can call my own.

Might not be tomorrow
Or next week,
Or next month,
Or next year.

But I'm strivin' to make it.
For now,
Till the time comes,
It'll come.

ELECTRIFYING • DISCOVERY

Yes,
I'll fight with every breath,
To make my story known.
Dominatin' every long day and night.

In this fight,
I will win.

No,
I won't give into this darkness,
I'll make the lights bright.
It's time to stand up,
There's no way back down.

ELECTRIFYING • DISCOVERY

I can't give up,
no matter what happens.

I'll never run away from
what's in front of me.

I won't close my eyes and hope.
I'll take chances
because of the future me in me.

ELECTRIFYING • DISCOVERY

My wounds have healed without scars.

They've been healed by your grace.
So when darkness comes,
and life moves so slow,
stay with me til the very end.

Promise me.

ELECTRIFYING • DISCOVERY

Discover your piece of story.

With full hearted and sincerity,
Bloomin' with grace of thoughts and emotions,
To discover your purpose to find.

ELECTRIFYING • DISCOVERY

Protect your energy and cells.

And,
limit the nervousness in your system.

ELECTRIFYING • DISCOVERY

Turnin' one connection
into millions of neural networks.

ELECTRIFYING • DISCOVERY

Keep your clique tight,
and bundled like nerve fibers.

ELECTRIFYING • DISCOVERY

Our world is changin'
Evolvin' towards the new.

This new world,
I've been holdin' back my darkest thoughts,
holdin' back my courage,
and holdin' back myself.

But you make me feel like
I can finally evolve with the world.

ELECTRIFYING • DISCOVERY

You are a gift from the Universe.

You are
excudin' compassion,
radiatin' a magical energy,
flourishin' in and out.

Remember,
you have a divine purpose.
Your purpose and power are within you.

Let it find you.

ELECTRIFYING • DISCOVERY

No options.

You're the only one I'm interested in discoverin' life with.

E L E C T R I F Y I N G • D I S C O V E R Y

Mid to late 20's,
a couple years of uncertainty and loneliness,
yet full of self-discovery and growth.

You might in a dark place,
in the same daily routine,
wanderin' the same road early mornings and late evenings.

No one tellin' you what to do with your life,
friends and colleagues gettin' engaged and married.

You're stuck and lost,
single and lonely.
Figurin' things out day and night,
But that's okay.

You have the power to switch your life around.

ELECTRIFYING • DISCOVERY

The grass might be greener on the other side.

That's why,
I'm choosin' to see the beauty on the other side.

ELECTRIFYING • DISCOVERY

In my new era,
I'm leavin' all the darkness in the shadow.
I'm makin' space for balanced and aligned energies,
awakenin' my intuitive self.

In my new era,
I'm obsessed with becomin' the
most beautiful and empowerin' goddess,
who is gentle, yet fierce
powerful, yet graceful
grounded, yet nurturin'.

I'm brave for my next electrifyin' era.

T | H

CAFFEINATED FLOW

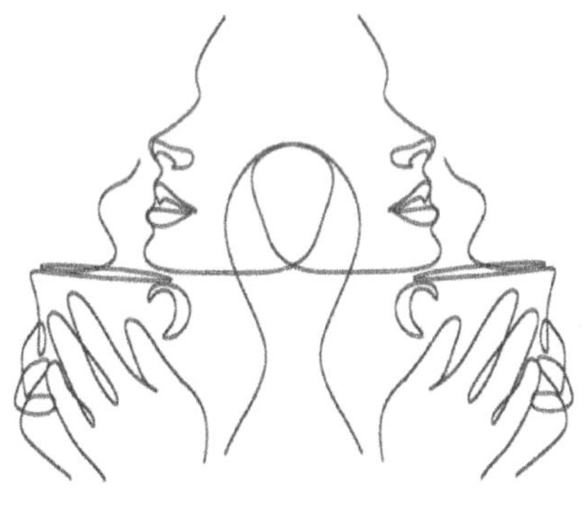

CAFFEINATED • FLOW

Guilty of lovin' coffee,
Addicted to coffee.
Coffee every hour
on the hour.

This is the secret to a breezy mornin'
and good night's sleep.

CAFFEINATED • FLOW

Heart poundin' in your chest,
busy days guarantee
no sleep.

Takin' caffeine shots
and wrestlin' thoughts,
just to make it out
in the world like the rest.

CAFFEINATED • FLOW

Fill my cup,
I'm on a mission.

Let's drink up the overflowin' cup,
full of love,
caffeine,
and adrenaline.

Ready to take your ambition
on the next mission?

CAFFEINATED • FLOW

In the mornin'
I pray for a strong caffeinated cup of coffee,
with love and courage,
with extra strength,
to dominate the battle of the day.

Cause I'll never know
what's life is bringin' me today.

CAFFEINATED • FLOW

Caffeine is keepin' me awake.

I keep stayin' up all night,
Scrollin' online,
Swipin' right
at least one more time.

Seekin' for that perfect match.

CAFFEINATED • FLOW

I know there's a thousand reasons that I should stop,
stop the adrenaline,
stop the addiction,
and stop the mission.

But I'm in too deep
into the flow.
It's not easy to stop it now.

CAFFEINATED • FLOW

I can feel the heat,
flushin' through your veins.

The ground,
shakin' with that java grindin' purpose of yours.

Now,
take a shot,
a shot of courage
a shot into the unknown,
and a shot or two of caffeine with me.

CAFFEINATED • FLOW

Let me drink you up.
I'm cravin' your energy.
It's runnin' through my veins.

You get my heart throbbin' with pure beats,
flowin' through my bloodstream.
I feel the affections in sip of love,
I'm lovin' how it all tastes down in my system
With warmth,
richness,
and boldness.

Makin' my adrenal glands pumpin' out adrenaline
and dilatin' my pupils.

C A F F E I N A T E D • F L O W

We're both addicted
to each other.

Coffee,
you and me.

We can work it out.
Meet me tomorrow at noon.

CAFFEINATED • FLOW

Caffeinate your mind,
body,
and soul.

So you can flow
through the 9-5's.

CAFFEINATED • FLOW

The city has been up all night with us.
Tellin' the youths to
"...stay in school, do what your told".

It's so hard,
when you know your lives on hold.

But at least we found each other,
each other's passion and goal,
each other's vision and support system.

That's something I won't ever let go.

CAFFEINATED • FLOW

No one knows what you've been through.

Time tickin' too rapidly,
for them to know.

Day by day,
drip by drip,
will ease you through your hardship.

CAFFEINATED • FLOW

Chargin' my phone and checkin' my email,
Strugglin' to find a meanin' in my soul.

But when I caffeinate,
I carry the weight of the world on my shoulders.

When I caffeinate,
I find more passion and love around me.

When I caffeinate,
I care only about thing that really matters.

CAFFEINATED • FLOW

There's emotion in every mornin' dark roasted cup
Keepin' me goin' everyday.
Goin' to work just to feel alive.

But what am I *really* livin' for?

I just want to take some time for myself
to refuel,
and feel renewed.

CAFFEINATED • FLOW

You came into my life
without hesitation.

You awakened me to a world
where I could energize.

CAFFEINATED • FLOW

I now know what I'm livin' for.

Livin' for
2 shots of espresso
with oatmilk
drizzled with caramel
in my iced caramel latte.

Livin' for
inner happiness,
advocatin' for others,
changes in healthcare,
and for buildin' an empire to raise my future gen in.

It all starts within me.
I found my own fulfillment,
Inner peace,
Confidence,
And happiness within me.

CAFFEINATED • FLOW

Take a sip of
bold,
adrenaline-rich,
and sweet
iced carmel latte.

Feel revived,
It's getting' easier.
Reality is gettin' clearer,
To your destination.
What you find and want,
It's deep in the cup of coffee.

CAFFEINATED • FLOW

One cup,
two cups
three cups anticipatin'.

Four hours,
five hours,
six more hours left to go.

CAFFEINATED • FLOW

Fill your cup with freshly ground beans,
make new paths with every drink.

Don't let your cup go empty,
ask for a refill
and take control of your life.

Be inspired to take control of life once more.

C A F F E I N A T E D • F L O W

One cup of story,
You poured for me.

Two cups of work,
Just to keep me sane.

Three cups of love,
is what I need.

Four cups of family and friends,
is the reason I keep hustlin' everyday.

CAFFEINATED • FLOW

Pourin' boldness,
Strength and love into this cup.

Hopes and dreams tasted by the tongues of youth,
Dizzle with carmel and sweet foam of dedication.

Ice caramel latte with passion,
resilience,
and self-fulfillment.

CAFFEINATED • FLOW

Matcha latte,
Pushin' the overload away.
9 to 5 completed workdays,
It's time for the next,
Next big check.

I'm addicted to success.
Matcha latte,
Makin' me work at my best.

C A F F E I N A T E D • F L O W

When the pre's hittin'
I'm grindin' at the gym,
That's my home.

Doin' pilates and high intensity workouts.
Lovin' the sweat,
Lovin' the burn,
Lovin' the winnin' progress 5-6x a week.
Keeps me movin'
Keeps me groovin'.

My life's not for the weak.

CAFFEINATED • FLOW

Jazz music harmonizin' throughout the kitchen,
smoky, nutty, aroma scent of espresso
fillin' up the cozy room.

Sittin' next to you early morning in silence.
So peaceful,
so comfortin'.

Your peace and comfort,
truly makes our nest feels more home-y.

CAFFEINATED • FLOW

Mornings are gettin' rough,
Gettin' up out of bed has become so hard,
Drinkin' coffee is just a must,
Still on a rush figurin' out
the next must.

CAFFEINATED • FLOW

No IV Therapy needed.

Bloodstream already gushin' with
Hazelnut Coffee and Taro Boba Milk Tea.

CAFFEINATED • FLOW

Sunday flow,
weekend always on the go.

Munching away Korean BBQ with family,
drinkin' up Lychee soju with friends,
and makin' plans for the next week with me.

Lovin' the flow to
how my typical weekend flows.

CAFFEINATED • FLOW

I can't remember the last time
I didn't crave for a taste that is
so intensely bold,
bitter-sweet,
chocolate-y,
and lovin'.

All the caffeine in the world,
but your affection is more caffeinated
than the strongest coffee in my kitchen.

UNCONDITIONAL LOVE

U N C O N D I T I O N A L • L O V E

Everywhere I look,
I check for your name on the list.
Everywhere I go,
you're the one on my mind.
I can't stop this feelin',
that's growin' inside.

All the little things
you do in life,
I'm followin' your footstep from a far.
Guidin' me on the same journey you're on.
I'm out here,
hopin' to cross your path again,
but you're a million miles far.

Maybe one day we'll reconnect and get things right.
Maybe another day,
but not today.

U N C O N D I T I O N A L • L O V E

Surely love and passion
can cure most things.
Healin' hands and soul
can change all things.

Find your inner doctor and save yourself,
Keep givin' love,
givin' life
so, you can make it out there another life.

UNCONDITIONAL • LOVE

No matter where you are tonight,
I'm with you.

Sending you unconditional
love from afar.

Sending you the blood cell
that flows from home
to your heart and lungs.

U N C O N D I T I O N A L • L O V E

The night is slow,
and the moon's hangin' over me.

They tell me that time heals,
only time is hard to find.

I need a new miracle,
tonight under this moonlight.

U N C O N D I T I O N A L • L O V E

You never appreciate what you want,
until you know exactly what you had.

The truth is then revealed,
you don't understand what you 'had' until it's gone.

U N C O N D I T I O N A L • L O V E

What we had was real.

Something so sweet and true,
brighter than a million stars.

But now,
that real moment seems like a dimmin' star,
a million of miles afar.

U N C O N D I T I O N A L • L O V E

If I am your doctor
let me care for you.

It's a true love and my vow to you,
I will never forget who I am bound to serve,
I will never forget who needs me in time of need.

So let me heal you.

U N C O N D I T I O N A L • L O V E

Each day feels like
the sunlight is stronger on my skin.

The sunlight is burnin'
Makin' me glow when I don't have to.
But at least
I'm no longer dark and cold.

I learned to be warm and lovin' again.
There's something special about
this new way I'm feelin',
No longer with the cold and the rain in me.
A new wind is blowin' as
I'm comin' out of the storm,
now glowin' with the sunlight.

UNCONDITIONAL • LOVE

Forgiveness is where I am from.
It is my inner home.

I am from forgiveness.

U N C O N D I T I O N A L • L O V E

There's a light in me again.

The broken dimly lit candle that I used to not find,
is now burnin' brighter
and not burnt out.

UNCONDITIONAL • LOVE

She hasn't seen you in so long.

Ever since you separated our puzzle pieces,
She is still findin' pieces of your heart
on the coffee table in her dinin' room.

Only there as a decoration
and not to put the puzzle pieces together.

UNCONDITIONAL • LOVE

I know I may not be perfect,
But I am worth it.

I see me the same way you want to see me,
I am the best thing that's ever happened to you and me.
I know I am rare and full of love.
All I need is happenin' for me.

UNCONDITIONAL • LOVE

Constantly lookin' in mirrors,
checkin' your reflection.

Whoa,
do you not like what you see?
You always find flaws in you,
That others cannot see.

Sometimes it's hard to be gentle on yourself,
it's hard not to look at the reflection starin' back at you.

Look back at the reflection
and start fallin' in love with you.

Cause only you deserve all the love
reflected to you from the world.

U N C O N D I T I O N A L • L O V E

All it takes is one swipe,
one swipe to the right,
and it's a match!

You reachin' out,
we connectin',
lovebombin' back and forth,
brunchin' and dinnin' round after rounds.

Round one,
the interview session.
Round two,
the chemistry test,
Round three,
the major baseball leagues.

Three strikes,
We're back to stranger.
Back again on the app.
Is this how we seekin' for true love nowadays?

UNCONDITIONAL • LOVE

What broke you and what healed you?
What made you want to live again?
What kind of happiness are you seekin' for?
What changed your mind?

The battle you fought,
it made you strong.

Answers are neither right nor wrong.
So, be the answer to all my questions.

UNCONDITIONAL • LOVE

Don't fall for the exterior design.

Fall for the interior values,
the story and history
that crafts the home true uniqueness.

U N C O N D I T I O N A L • L O V E

Unconditional love,
the greatest housewarmin' gift you can receive in a lifetime.

It's a gift from the Universe,
lettin' you know that
you are loveable,
you are deserving of romance,
and you are irreplaceable.

Welcome home,
welcome unconditional love into your home.

U N C O N D I T I O N A L • L O V E

Scrollin' through the 'gram,
Checkin' the timeline,
Lookin' up to see how you're doin' life lately,
Just tryin' to figure out where you are.

Whoa,
The new photo you posted,
The new story you shared,
I don't recognize you anymore.
You're smilin',
But I can see sadness in your eyes.
You're out there livin' a life we once dreamed about.
Not bitter,
Just truly happy for you.

I'll be okay.

UNCONDITIONAL • LOVE

It's been so long.
We've been apart for so long.

Reminiscin' about good ole times,
and events that could've manifested.

U N C O N D I T I O N A L • L O V E

Let's go on a road trip.

Let's roam the Earth,
escape the fantasy
and land in paradise.

Within a heartbeat,
put you on top,
with your eyes are mesmerizin'
as we're explorin' from the moon to sun,
back and forth.

One night of passion,
one touch of love,
one trip to the Universe.

You're my wanderlust.

155
T | H

CARDIAC • FEELINGS

CARDIAC • FEELINGS

Well,
Here I am.

Turnin' feelings into thoughts,
thoughts into words,
words into writings,
and writings into stories.

Stories and secrets that I won't get to tell you,
but will be published
and eventually one day you'll read it.

One day,
you'll read the legacy that I left behind.

C A R D I A C • F E E L I N G S

If you feel out of place and like an outsider,
Believe me when I say
that every single person in this world has felt that way.

If you ever feel like your opinions don't matter,
and your voice doesn't count,
It doesn't make you less valuable as a human being,
It makes you more valuable for experiencin' and
feelin' those things.

C A R D I A C • F E E L I N G S

She'lll truly love someone
with every heartbeat in her if
Someone who loves her for who she is
and for who she can be,
Someone who won't hurt her and try to break her happiness,
Someone who opens the curtains of life for her,
showin' her all the possibilities that she could achieve every
mornin'
showin' her all your true self,
your heart of gold,
your compassion,
your loyalty.

And your promise to her.

CARDIAC • FEELINGS

There was a time when I wanted someone,
And he wanted everybody.

But now,
I just want no one.

CARDIAC • FEELINGS

Nostalgia was settin' in the other lonely night.

But tonight,
It's a new feelin' of fresh air
and new beginnings.

CARDIAC • FEELINGS

The other day I gave myself a lil pep talk.

Thinkin' about a change,
Findin' myself in my reflection,
Learnin' about who I am,
And lovin' all the flaws that built me
for who I am.

CARDIAC • FEELINGS

What emotions do you really feel?

Are you lost and numb?
Searchin' for something' or someone?
Fragmented in your reality,
Tryin' to keep your head up,
But the pressure,
The pressure is buildin' up your heart walls.

C A R D I A C • F E E L I N G S

I was lookin' for love
but keep feelin' numb.

Saw a lot of faces,
but there's never been a hint of feelings.

I was lookin' for love
but keep feelin' numb.
Maybe I should stop the time
and stop lookin'.

C A R D I A C • F E E L I N G S

Many years have passed me by
since our last goodbyes.

I've seen a million people
and watched them come and go,
But some don't go,
they simply holdin' up the line.

It's been a long time
since our first hello.

CARDIAC • FEELINGS

Continue findin' peace
in all the broken hearts.

Healthy destiny in these fragments of your soul,
Soon you'll find the valley of tranquility and peace,
All in one piece.

C A R D I A C • F E E L I N G S

It's Saturday night,
everyone across the world is out
seekin' for that someone,
but I'm comfortably at home.

I'm not going out tonight.
Givin' my time to myself and no one else.

The wind is blowin' cool and crisp,
I'm in my bed,
Cozyin' up with a book and a mug of hot chocolate.

Ooh,
I love this peaceful feelin' tonight.

C A R D I A C • F E E L I N G S

Romantic spark,
it could mean something.

Tell me how it feels to have that spark between us again.

C A R D I A C • F E E L I N G S

I'm your Queen.

Treat me like you care,
Protect me at all costs,
Dedicate your entire life to me.

CARDIAC • FEELINGS

You see the whole world in her.

Tryin' to resist' the urge to look into her eyes,
can't help feelin' the magnetic force pullin' you closer,
dreamin' of her everynight,
searchin' for stars to align the skylight.

Her beautiful attraction is lightin' up this world
and pullin' you closer into her world.

C A R D I A C • F E E L I N G S

I put my arms around you
as you put your words around me.

Givin' each other the faith,
patience
and reassurance we need.

Cause once upon a time,
someone did not do it for me.

CARDIAC • FEELINGS

Seenin' the glimpse of you from afar,
Taller, muscular, more attractive than before.
The memories rushin' back,
the seductive voice whispherin'
the passion and spark,
that was once there.

Suddenly,
I feel the adrenaline runnin' through my veins,
adrenaline rushin',
and the thrillin' moment again.

It's a sudden rush of adrenaline
in heart and throughout the bones
to start feelin' this feelin' again.

C A R D I A C • F E E L I N G S

Though love is not always as
smooth like butter,
sweet like sugar,
or spicy like chili,
I've not given up on the perfect love that I dreamed.

C A R D I A C • F E E L I N G S

Eventually,
You'll be my King.

You'll be the light of my day
as I step into the castle.

Be my King and
I'll treat you like the King you deserve.

C A R D I A C • F E E L I N G S

Love is more than
the 3 words (I Love You),
the make-up pleasure after an argument,
the handful of apologies and phrases
that you say over and over.

C A R D I A C • F E E L I N G S

Love builds romantically over time
through trust,
understanding,
patience,
communication,
and vulnerability.

CARDIAC • FEELINGS

Timin' was never wrong.

We were never meant to be right
for each other.

CARDIAC • FEELINGS

You're a blessin',
an angel from above.

You deserve the
bless of me.

CARDIAC • FEELINGS

Home is so much more,
more than a fancy mansion in a distant land.

That's truly the home that is worth
investin' your future generation in.

CARDIAC • FEELINGS

The key to the gates of heaven can be found in your heart.

Home is for everyone to find.
So come on,
find where you belong.

ADRENALINE-RICH JOURNEY

A D R E N A L I N E - R I C H • J O U R N E Y

Don't fear your own inconsistencies.

Genuinely power through the uncertainty of life.
Holdin' up close to existentialist principles and ideas.

When you're in the darkness,
there's always someone
or something
shinin' brighter than you
to help you navigate through.

ADRENALINE-RICH • JOURNEY

Excitement doesn't last long.

Caught up in routine and nonsense,
things you don't actually care about.
Cause every moment,
you count your blessings.

ADRENALINE-RICH • JOURNEY

I was lookin' for a way to fill emptiness.
It was an emptiness that
no one else would understand.

People told me to find new batteries,
But I found those old ones still charged up
just the right amount
for my emptiness.

ADRENALINE-RICH • JOURNEY

Find a friend or soulmate
that carries you as a passenger.

A lover or an active listener
that will keep you sane.

Whoever listens and hears you,
understands your drive.

Find passion and purpose
surroundin' those
in you.

ADRENALINE-RICH • JOURNEY

I'm boss of my life.,
I can command this next phase of my life
to be the most fulfillin'.
Cause each and every day is a better chapter
written in my story.

Show me the beauty of life for me to see
and shake off all the fears I've been facin'.

ADRENALINE-RICH • JOURNEY

The heart is your inner compass
that points you to your life's purpose.

When you follow its guidance,
you will find the path to your life adventure.

ADRENALINE-RICH • JOURNEY

A compassionate heart is
the medicine you need.

When life gets tough,
and you start to bleed,
it's the heart that knows what you
truly need.

And it's the heart that will
lead us to our purpose in life.

Trust your heart,
and let it guide you
on the journey
you were meant to love livin' for.

ADRENALINE-RICH • JOURNEY

I am never lettin' the light dim again,
I am burstin' with passion and joy to the core.

The doubts,
background noises
and the question of uncertainties,
are now fadin' away.

A D R E N A L I N E - R I C H • J O U R N E Y

Met you in Physics,
but our chemistry bond was incredibly intense.
What we had,
made it seem so perfect.

Too perfect to be true.

We used to talk about places we wanted to explore,
dreams we wanted to create.
I remember all those good times,
all the moments we've shared.

After college,
we said our last goodbyes,
took our last graduation pictures together,
went our separate paths.

Your name,
poppin' in my mind throughout times.
But you settled
and I've moved on.
Hope you found me in your person,
and that you're truly happy out there.

A D R E N A L I N E - R I C H • J O U R N E Y

Lock the door that no longer serve you,
no longer serve your purpose,
no longer serve your worth,
no longer serve your love.

So,
let the next door
open a grand entrance of possibilities.

ADRENALINE-RICH • JOURNEY

We're ridin' on a different road.

You go your way,
I'll go my way.

My way's
leadin' me home.

ADRENALINE-RICH • JOURNEY

I knew at the time,
it wasn't worth the rush.

When the high's high,
the low's low.

Now,
I'm concentratin' on
doin' good for my soul.

ADRENALINE-RICH • JOURNEY

It's time to do somethin' for me.

Time to relax in a peaceful sauna,
time to soak up in mineral mud mask,
and time to scrub out all the negativity off my skin.

It's time to wash away the tangled,
longin' desire
and breath in a healin' of Eucalyptus air.

ADRENALINE-RICH • JOURNEY

This great unknown is waitin' for you,
Beyond what you have seen.

Let the unknown be soon known.

A D R E N A L I N E - R I C H • J O U R N E Y

As the adventure of life unfolds,
I'm just on this journey.

A journey of exploration...no real destination,
meetin' new people along the way,
and hopin' they might stay.

ADRENALINE-RICH • JOURNEY

Continue workin' on yourself.

Work on your personality,
work on findin' your passion,
work on gettin' the bags,
and work on fulfillin' your own dreams.

Work on yourself
'til others work for you.

A D R E N A L I N E - R I C H • J O U R N E Y

To all the doors that locked me out,
I'm comin' back to open a grand entrance.

To all the people that let me go,
I'm comin' back as your idol.

We'll meet again,
soon.

ADRENALINE-RICH • JOURNEY

Growin' up as an independent daughter,
Growin' and flourishin' my whole life,
Livin' freely and bloomin' wildly.

ADRENALINE-RICH • JOURNEY

Pamper your life.

Wash away all your concerns and worries,
head straight to paradise,
relaxin' tonight in the jacuzzi pool.

ADRENALINE-RICH • JOURNEY

Though my destination is still unknown,
I'm still learnin' from experiences.

I'm grateful for everythin' right now,
It is what I need it to be.

I'm grateful 'cause
there are so many forces drivin' me forward,
grateful for these good vibes I'm feelin' that surround me,
grateful for another beautiful day and night,
and I'm grateful for the Universe support and miracles
guidin' my journey.

ADRENALINE-RICH • JOURNEY

Discoverin' life's blessings instead of pain,
Blessings and miracles from the darkest days,
For all the sweet highs and lows,
Openin' up a new way for the grand show.

ADRENALINE-RICH • JOURNEY

I want to be your first.

First glimpse you take in the morning,
First call on your emergency contact,
First Queen standin' beside you,
First lifetime investment,
First true love.

Let me be your first in this lifetime.

ADRENALINE-RICH • JOURNEY

Empty out your old coffee.
Drain away all the
old habits,
old, fixed mindsets,
old, comforting routines.

Refill up your empty cup
with new growth mindsets,
new experiences,
new connections,
new visions in life.

Remember,
Add cream and values into this cup of coffee
for a sweet and adrenaline journey.

ADRENALINE-RICH • JOURNEY

When your fears are close,
Amidst the uncertainty you feel,
No matter the trials and tribulations,
You are still worthy of miracles.

A D R E N A L I N E - R I C H • J O U R N E Y

Ooh,
Livin' in this city with a high-rise view.

Keeps my mind completely innovative,
thinkin' about life from the view up here.
Used to dream about this day,
but now I'm lovin' this new scene.

I appreciate the place I now live in,
livin life like there's no tomorrow.

ADRENALINE-RICH • JOURNEY

Teach me,
all the process in this journey.

Show me,
your support.

Tell me,
your words of affirmations.

Mentor me,
throughout life.

ADRENALINE-RICH • JOURNEY

All roads led to a different home.

I found my home,
found my peace,
found my inner happiness.

Most importantly,
I found myself.

I have found everything,
but I will still not unpack
and settle.

A D R E N A L I N E - R I C H • J O U R N E Y

I was sittin' on my porch thinkin' about the things,
that happened to me 10 years ago.

Thinkin' about where I am today,
how could it have gone so right?

I'm sittin' on my porch everyday now,
laughin' and reminiscin' at all the things that I went through.

So happy that the past is now behind me.

A D R E N A L I N E - R I C H • J O U R N E Y

There's a new change happenin' in you.

Eternally livin',
Bloomin' wild inside you.

The details of your future,
all that you know,
is callin' for you to bloom.

ADRENALINE-RICH • JOURNEY

You've had enough excuses,
it's time to make a choice.

You're tougher than you know,
you're stronger than you see,
and you're smarter than you think.

Be your own role model
that you inspire to be.

A D R E N A L I N E - R I C H • J O U R N E Y

You've what it takes to build your empire.

Buildin' the land of courage,
land of hope,
land of boldness,
through this construction journey.

There's a new land developin'
But you're not afraid of the development,
You won't be knocked down,
Soon,
you'll be queenin' as the new homeowner
in this empire.

ADRENALINE-RICH • JOURNEY

Live the best life you can live
instead of settlin' for what was given to you.

Now is your time.

TRULY HOME